Spy Kid

MAKING SPY DISGUISES

Deanna Caswell

BLACK
RABBIT
BOOKS

Hi Jinx is published by Black Rabbit Books
P.O. Box 3263, Mankato, Minnesota, 56002.
www.blackrabbitbooks.com
Copyright © 2019 Black Rabbit Books

Marysa Storm, editor; Michael Sellner, designer;
Grant Gould, production designer;
Omay Ayres, photo researcher

Library of Congress Cataloging-in-Publication Data
Names: Caswell, Deanna, author.
Title: Making spy disguises / by Deanna Caswell.
Description: Mankato, Minnesota : Black Rabbit Books,
2019. | Series: Hi jinx. Spy kid | Includes bibliographical
references and index.
Identifiers: LCCN 2017055216 (print) | LCCN 2018013918
(ebook) | ISBN 9781680725933 (e-book) | ISBN
9781680725872 (library binding) | ISBN 9781680727418
(paperback)
Subjects: LCSH: Espionage–Equipment and supplies–Juvenile
literature. | Disguise–Juvenile literature.
Classification: LCC UB270.5 (ebook) | LCC UB270.5 .C377 2019
(print) | DDC 327.12–dc23
LC record available at https://lccn.loc.gov/2017055216

Printed in the United States. 4/18

Image Credits

Alamy: Nano Calvo, 10–11; iStock: A-Digit, 4 (restaurant);
Agustinc, Cover (spy, city bkgd), 2–3, 4 (bkgd), 8 (spy), 11
(spy); Alexandr III, 3; dedMazay, 1; SensorSpot, 19 (man);
Thodoris_Tibilis, 8 (glass), 10 (glass), 13 (glass), 14 (glass),
17 (glass), 18 (glass); Shutterstock: Artens, 14–15; Basjan
Bernard, 11 (bttm); BLACKDAY, 19 (top); Christos Georghiou,
4 (Marine); Freestyle_stock_photo, 11 (bkgd); inklisem, Cover
(starry bkgd); Laia Design Studio, 19 (teeth); Lemonade
Serenade, Cover (bttm); Memo Angeles, 4 (woman, banker),
NikomMaelao Production, Cover (moon); NotionPic, 15;
opicobello, 13 (torn paper); Pasko Maksim, Back Cover (top),
23, 24; Pitju, 19 (page curl), 21 (page curl); Ron Dale, 5, 9,
13 (top), 20; sailormoon, 8 (try it), 10 (try it), 13 (try it),
14 (try it), 17 (try it), 18 (try it); stegworkz, 12, 21 (person);
studiostoks, 16; Valery Sidelnykov, 6–7; Vector Tradition SM,
11 (eyes), 22–23 Every effort has been made to contact copyright
holders for material reproduced in this book. Any omissions
will be rectified in subsequent printings if notice is given to
the publisher.

CONTENTS

CHAPTER 1

Undercover............5

CHAPTER 2

Quick Changes........9

CHAPTER 3

Creating a Cover......13

CHAPTER 4

Get in on the Hi Jinx. .20

Other Resources. 22

UNDERCOVER

The agent scoots into a restaurant booth. A rip in the seat hides a message. He checks for one every Monday. Same booth, same rip. But the agent looks different each time. Last Monday, he dressed as a young Marine. He had a uniform and mustache. Today, he's a plump banker. His padded suit makes him sweaty. Next time, he'll be an old woman who walks with a cane.

Top Secret

Spy missions can be dangerous. Agents might need disguises to hide their **identities**. They must walk around without their enemies catching them. Spies use many techniques to blend in. So can you!

Chapter 2

QUICK CHANGES

Sometimes spies just need quick, simple disguises. They only need to hide their **features**. Hats, coats, and glasses work well. People can't see their important features, such as hair and eye color.

Spies **avoid** flashy disguises. The last thing they want to do is draw attention to themselves.

Find a few hats and glasses. Get out some thick hoodies or borrow some coats. Find a combination that hides your features but doesn't stand out. That's the best disguise. Throw it on to quickly hide your identity.

Posture and Walk

For a quick disguise, spies don't just change what they wear. They change how they move. People notice how someone stands and walks. To throw off enemies and protect their identities, spies change their movements.

There are many ways to change how you walk. Put a pebble in one of your shoes.

Or wear the wrong shoe size.

You can also take shorter or longer steps. Keep your changes small and simple. A big limp will draw attention to you!

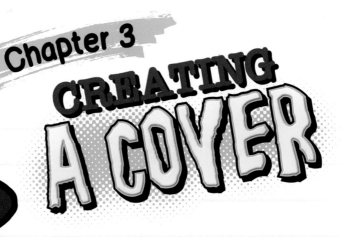

Chapter 3
CREATING A COVER

On some missions, spies need more than quick disguises. Instead, they need whole new identities. These new identities are called covers. Covers are full disguises. They include everything from the way spies look to how they live. Spies live as completely different people to gather information.

Make up a cover for yourself. Give your cover a name and backstory. Where is your cover from? What's your new family like? Give your cover hobbies and interests too. Make a list of these traits. Your cover should be believable.

Getting Dressed

A spy's cover has his or her own style. The spy wears clothes that make sense for the part he or she is playing. A spy's cover also has to blend in with his or her environment.

Think about your cover, and look at your list of traits. What kind of clothes should you wear? Should you wear athletic clothes? Or maybe nice, fancy outfits are better?

Speech and Behavior

Undercover spies talk differently than they normally would. They avoid their usual phrases. Their covers use different ones. If a spy often says, "For sure," he might start saying, "Definitely."

A spy gives his or her cover different habits too. Some covers pick at their nails. Others might play with their hair.

How would your cover talk? Try out some new phrases, such as "Sweet!" or "No way!" Try out new habits too. Look around when you talk. Rattle coins in your pocket, or stare at the floor.

Makeup

Makeup is a spy's best friend.
Spies use it to change their features.
They add wrinkles or moles to their
faces. Fake teeth change their looks.
Fake facial hair and wigs help too.

Find some makeup pencils.
Use them to darken your
eyebrows. Or use them
to give yourself freckles.
Little changes are best.

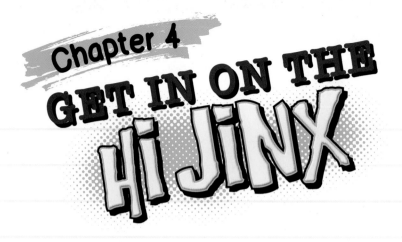

Chapter 4

GET IN ON THE Hi JiNX

Spies aren't the only ones who use disguises. Animals do too! Many animals go undercover as plants or parts of their **habitats**. These disguises keep them hidden from **predators**.

Some animals disguise themselves as other creatures. The mimic octopus pretends to be a deadly sea snake or poisonous fish to scare away predators. One type of moth pretends to be a **venomous** wasp. Hungry animals are sure to stay away from it! Nature is full of animal disguises. Look to them for **inspiration**.

Take It One Step More

1. Do you think it's OK to trick people with disguises? Why or why not?

2. Which changes in this book would be easy to make? Which changes would be hard? Why?

3. What do spy disguises and animal disguises have in common? How are they different?

GLOSSARY

avoid (uh-VOID)—to keep away from

feature (FEE-chur)—an interesting or important part or quality

habitat (HAB-uh-tat)—the place where a plant or animal grows or lives

identity (ahy-DEN-ti-tee)—who someone is

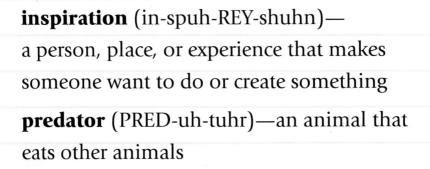

inspiration (in-spuh-REY-shuhn)— a person, place, or experience that makes someone want to do or create something

predator (PRED-uh-tuhr)—an animal that eats other animals

trait (TREYT)—a characteristic or quality

venomous (VEN-uh-mus)—containing venom or poison

BOOKS

Caswell, Deanna. *Mastering Spy Techniques.* Spy Kid. Mankato, MN: Black Rabbit Books, 2019.

Kallen, Stuart A. *World War II Spies and Secret Agents.* Heroes of World War II. Minneapolis: Lerner Publications, 2018.

Larson, Kirsten W. *The CIA.* Protecting Our People. Mankato, MN: Amicus High Interest, 2017.

WEBSITES

KidSpy Zone
www.spymuseum.org/education-programs/kids-families/kidspy-zone/

Kids' Zone
https://www.cia.gov/kids-page

Spy Disguises – Dress Up and Be Someone Else
www.topspysecrets.com/spy-disguises.html

INDEX

A

animals, 20

C

clothing, 9, 11, 14

covers, 13, 14, 17

H

habits, 17

M

makeup, 18

P

posture, 10–11

S

speech and behavior, 17